First Love Many Times

First Love Many Times

KAPIL RAJ

Anecdote
Publishing House

Anecdote
Publishing House

Anecdote Publishing House
E-35-A, E Block, Gali No. 2, Ganesh Nagar,
Pandav Nagar Complex, Delhi - 110092

Published by Anecdote Publishing House

First Edition 2023

ISBN: 9788195890729

MRP: ₹ 149.00

Book Promoted and Marketed by Champ Readers Pvt. Ltd.

Layout and Cover by Anecdote
Printed in India

*To all the free souls,
hurt, chained, and caged
by social rules and
fabrications*

Change Stories by

Kapil Raj

Change Stories by Kapil Raj is an amalgamation of five independent short stories: ***Kuroopa, A Gutterful Life, First Love Many Times, Flying with Chains, and A Mother By The Window.***

Advancement of humankind invariably poses new challenges to the existing social order in society. It weakens the bondages enforced by patriarchal rules, paving the way for societal awakening. However, every ounce of progress leaves behind some debris in its wake. Failure to recognise this debris or 'problem' can bestow acute misery and suffering in the lives of people. Going back and snipping the problem in the bud is usually more cumbersome than revolting and moving forward.

If only there was an easy way out.

True social development cannot be achieved without breaking existing stereotypes and adapting our mindsets to the subsequent changes.

Each short story interweaves a heartening story with a deeply imbibed social issue, hardened public belief, and associated fabrications. As you read the narrative, you watch and evolve with the characters, sometimes feeling yourself in them – empathising in circumstances that may or may not have existed in your lives. The stories will highlight the suffering that was never supposed to take place had we brought about a meaningful change for ourselves and others in the society.

However, there's always a first, and it can start here.

We live how we think, and we think how we choose to live.
Progress is hard; change is heroic.

Acknowledgements

Every beginning has a story. We often emphasise too much on the journey and the end goal, forgetting all about that *first step*.

When I commenced writing *ENDURER A Rape Story*, I was scared spending nights on the outcome. From the inception of the idea to getting the story published, three years passed. The book finally, reached the hands of readers and found love in a way I had never imagined.

For the first time, when I held the mic in a room full of young students to speak on the subject (rape and sexual assaults) which is considered one of the biggest taboo in the Indian households, my hands trembled, yet I took that leap.

By the end of each of session, I was gifted emotions, witnessed appreciation and respect. It was a dream come true. But a thought lingered behind. What next? What topic should I pick? Will I be able to justify the appreciation and recognition I received? The turmoil was too much. For a moment, I felt giving up. In those times, there are people who stand with you, influencing in ways which do not let yourself stop and take on unfamiliar paths.

They are my parents, my wife Payal, my sister Dimple and my son Hetarth. I owe you.

Pulkit, Thank You. You always stood along. When I simply could not progress further, your faith in me made me hold on and continue to move.

Tatiana, I am grateful for your persuasion and astute conversations. You incepted ideas on which I was able to write and build these stories.

Tina, you have my gratitude. You chiselled out the entire work with your editing and added a clear voice to the words.

Sincere thanks to Anecdote Publishers & Sagar Azad, who trusted me with my unconventional project and extended all support to get published.

And most importantly, I would like to thank all my readers. Your reviews, personal texts, praises and critiques motivated me to walk through this journey.

1

Dream or reality – what would you prefer? The former brings everlasting excitement and anticipation that is independent of the conclusion, whereas the latter is a strenuous, wakeful journey towards a bittersweet destination.

Abhi preferred to reach his destination by walking till the end of the road. He had dreamed about this moment for months. The majestic Taj Mahal stood proud and elegant against the backdrop of a sky radiant with innumerable colours and bespeckled with puffy clouds – it was truly a sight to behold.

He, a knight in shining armour, saunters with the girl of his dreams, Kavya. His imagination runs wild, adding and multiplying on the go. The exuberant gardens bore colourful flowers and delicate butterflies drifted in the balmy summer air, creating a dreamlike scenery. The artist would have left this world as a contented man except for one remaining bit – Kavya's reaction to what was about to transpire. It was Abhi's destiny to experience this spectacle in flesh and blood. This memory would live in his heart forever.

Before the ultimate moment, he soaked in the fresh air, pacifying his dipping confidence. Then he bent down before his muse. There is an enormous difference between planning and execution. Even after practising a hundred times, his anxiety refused to ebb and went through the roof. He could hear his heartbeat. The ecstatic expression of Kavya's that he had imagined vanished. However, he closed his eyes and took a deep breath, trusting the power of true love. Clutching a bouquet, he kept one foot ahead of the other and edged towards the love of his life. Such a proposal was unheard of in his circle, one that would become a talking point in many social events for years to come, its retelling transfers from one generation to the next. Suddenly, the dream ended, and reality surfaced.

Some well-rehearsed words left Abhi's lips, and a few struggled out of Kavya's. With a hidden letter, the bouquet struck Abhi's face and landed on the floor. A tear escaped from the depths of his heart, crossing a hoard of loving memories and shattering the pillars of hope. Abhi bent his head in humiliation. His shadow shone on his extremely polished shoes. Tender flowers lay scattered in the now scorching heat, bent with insult. His heart contracted with pain and disbelief, and tears gushed out of his eyes. He couldn't believe the events that had just transpired. The day was supposed to end in jubilation, not misery.

Kavya left, but the illusion of her presence still lingered. Abhi stared at the spot she just vacated. Tidal waves of shock plummeted through his body. He was numb from head to toe and had no awareness of his surroundings – he couldn't even tell if he was sitting or standing. He could hear the roar of laughter from the angels above. The spirit of Shah Jahan was holding his belly with hilarity.

The spot was not ordinary. The day was not mundane. Those flowers, that letter, the ink, those ribbons, each item had been chosen painstakingly to make the occasion special. A simple 'Yes' would have changed his life forever, filled with happiness and a promise of a better future. Instead, he had lost. It was like his life was over.

2

Abhi ignored his elder sister, who was constantly yelling at him for missing his tuition classes, and then locked himself in his room. After every couple of minutes, she would return and knock harder. Finally, on his mother's command, Abhi unlocked the door. His bloodshot eyes and perspiring forehead spoke for him and Mrs Sharma rushed to get him some medicine.

Despite the early afternoon, the temperature soared. Abhi gulped down an entire bottle of ice-cold water and allowed the fiery winds to blow on his face. This was the easiest way to fall sick considering his immunity – his bodily resistance to temperature changes was downright minimal. He needed some solace, which was impossible with his sister prancing around the room.

Shalini sensed her brother was faking this illness. Just that morning, she had spotted Abhi stealing money from their parents' room. She had been monitoring his actions since then. Extra shirts, salon treatments, a new pair of sunglasses were beyond the scope of his limited pocket money. There was something fishy going on; she was sure of it.

Mr Sharma was a senior manager at a bank and was always late to return home. Mrs Sharma, on the other hand, was quite invested in the boutique business she ran. This left it up to Shalini to keep a check on her younger brother and ensure he didn't run amok. Abhi had been behaving idiotically for the past few days. She had a hunch, but the discarded receipt of a recently purchased expensive pendant left no room for doubt – there was a girl involved. Shalini knew she was guilty of trespassing and rummaging through her brother's bag, but her actions were noble. Sometimes, one has to take the law into their hands to protect the law. She now had proof and just need to figure out who this girl was.

Mrs Sharma left, and for Abhi, Shalini's presence was nothing more than that of an irritating blood-sucking parasite. He often wished he never had a sibling. Within minutes of being left alone, there was always some kind of noise, shouting, things falling, curses flying about, but today there was silence.

"I know what you have been up to," said Shalini, expecting a reaction from Abhi.

Abhi ignored her and zoned out. He had no intention of replying to her.

"I know about the things you have been pilfering. Wait till dad finds out!" she shouted, throwing the receipt at his face.

The piece of paper jolted him out of his reverie and

landed him on planet Earth. Since that morning's incident, this was the first thing he paid attention to. He identified the printed slip and remembered the associated purchase. It was safely concealed in a unique handmade pocket inside his backpack. This meant –

"Did you…?" Abhi skimmed the receipt again in disbelief. He asked again, "Did you just open my bag and go through my stuff?"

"Don't try to make me the culprit here. You have been stealing for months and here is the proof," retorted Shalini.

Abhi trembled with rage; his eyes swelling with blood. He had had enough. Putting up with regular infringement of his privacy – like checking his phone calls, selection of friends, tabs on his whereabouts in and after school and even at home, monitoring his expenditures, school assignments – was one thing. Today, unfortunately, Shalini had crossed all limits and done the unthinkable – encroach on his fundamental rights as a human being. Abhi exploded without thinking about the outcome.

He threw the sheet off his body and bashed his fist on the side table, shaking the lamp that was placed on it. He got off the bed and stormed towards Shalini. Abhi's sudden reaction and leap towards her momentarily made her forget that he was her younger brother. Fear crept into her heart, and she stepped back. Abhi threw the receipt at her face and haphazardly grabbed the bag kept by her side. In his haste, he shoved Shalini by mistake and she fell on the floor. Ignoring her, he removed the pendant from the secret pocket and flung it at his sister. Luckily, it landed on her stomach.

"You girls are nothing but heartless devils!" he screamed, grabbing his shoes and smashing the door behind him as he left the room.

Shalini sat on the floor, shuddering with fear and shame. She had never seen this side of Abhi before. Maybe, her brother was not as young as she had thought.

3

Pulkit sneaked out of the tuition class from the back door hearing Abhi's whistle. After repeated attempts, the scooter finally gave up its resistance and started up. The boys rode in silence. Pulkit had been with Abhi from the beginning; he had witnessed all the humiliation. He had warned Abhi against Kavya, but still hoped the girl would give his friend a chance.

Kavya was one of the most popular girls in school. Her natural brown hair and hazel eyes shimmered in contrasting colours. Unlike many other girls, she didn't need to work on her appearance. After enrolling last year in this school, Kavya tried to make new friends but soon distanced herself after excessive attention from boys and negative publicity from the ones who got rejected got by her.

Out of all her admirers, Abhi had fared the best so far. His pleasing personality and non-stop jokes broke the ice right at the start. Soon they discovered common interests in orchestral music and artistic films. Kavya found a cure for her loneliness, but Abhi became spellbound by her charm. He would wake up thinking about her and sleep at night, wishing they were together forever. During one of their conversations, Kavya revealed she liked a boy in her last school, but he had stopped talking to her because of the long distance. Abhi was indifferent. He was confident he could win her over. True love happens once in a lifetime and he thought he had found it this time, just like in Shahrukh Khan's movies.

Abhi would do anything and everything for Kavya. From mobile recharges to assisting her in shopping, collecting clothes from the tailor, or finishing her assignments. He would steal glances at her whenever she sat next to a window, the air gently brushing her hair. A strange aura surrounded her. Her mere presence filled him with energy and happiness. He also went to her house once to repair her laptop. Soon these visits became a regular occurrence, and one day Kavya asked him to help shoot her videos for Instagram. Abhi took online courses for video and image editing and even rented a DSLR camera for shoots during the weekends.

The boys reached their regular hangout spot – a coffee shop. Pulkit went inside and returned with two mugs of cappuccino while Abhi waited next to the scooter.

"Do you know what is wrong with you?" asked Pulkit, waiting to see if Abhi would respond to his question.

"You are a good boy!" he continued when he received no reaction.

Abhi looked at Pulkit and just shrugged. Nothing seemed to make sense to him.

"Yes, my man. This is your problem – good guys

get their hearts broken. Sincerity, commitment, loyalty – these things are outdated now. Girls like 'bad boys' who treat them poorly. This, my friend, is the universal truth," said Pulkit.

Abhi's fist tightened.

"Look at you! You treated her like a queen, and she threw you aside like a fly in a cup. Tell me one thing she didn't make you do. What did she expect? Do guys run errands for every other girl? And now she'll make you suffer by saying, 'Oh, you broke my trust!' 'Oh, to me, you were just a friend!' I am telling you, buddy, we have to behave like grownups. We have to act bad and wicked. You know what I mean!" winked Pulkit, gesturing at a group of adults smoking outside the coffee shop.

There was no denying Pulkit's claim. These days the competition to acquire a girlfriend or boyfriend was stronger than acing the board exams. It's just the nerdy belt that studied hard because they knew their social skills were next to naught anyway and their chances of finding a partner in school, next to none. Abhi pondered on what Pulkit had just said and realised there was a lot of truth in his words.

Krish was the biggest liar of their batch, yet he was roaming around with two girls – one in school and another in tuition. He had the physique of a 12th grader and would randomly get into fights to show off his might. Rishit had his charm in deceiving people. Manmeet threw money at parties. And then there were the sincere ones who just listened and watched all the drama unfurl around them.

Unfortunately, Abhi was neither here nor there – he was stuck in the middle. He was funny, sufficiently popular in school, and loved Kavya earnestly. He was not there to satisfy his ego or roam around with a trophy girlfriend. Yes, he was too young. Still, he had given his heart away to a girl because his intentions were pure. But Kavya's reaction to his feelings had brought him to the question – what now?

4

Perplexed by his conversation with Pulkit, Abhi decided to walk back home. He couldn't get Kavya out of his mind. That innocent smile, wide enough to count her shiny teeth; those perfectly shaped eyebrows, raised playfully when she was up to some mischief. Whenever she placed a hand on his shoulder, the warmth of her touch sent tingles down his spine.

One time, after they were returning from a school picnic, Kavya sat beside Abhi. The bus rode through the early darkness of a wintery evening.

Tired from the day's frolic, she dozed off with her head lolling from side to side. Soon it fell on Abhi's shoulder. He could feel the warmth of her breath and the softness of her hair on his face. Subconsciously, his eyes fell on the window of the opposite seat. He gazed at his image with her. It appeared picture-perfect.

Yes, they looked like a couple! At that moment, he knew this was the girl he wanted to be with, forever. She was his soulmate. No matter what the future had in store for them, his every action henceforth would aspire to win her heart and ensure a happily ever after.

On his way back home, he crossed the society park. He entered it without thinking, just looking for an iota of peace. As he walked towards a bench, he noticed a hedge of flowers by the walkway. Remembering the morning's debacle, he stomped on them, crushing the flowers furiously. It was unwarranted, but he couldn't control his feelings. Suddenly, a thorn pricked his ankle. He shrieked, jumping up and down on the spot. A girl laughed from behind. Mahi walked up to him with a smile and plucked the thorn out of his foot.

“I guess you had a biting day,” she teased.

“Mind your own business!” yelled Abhi.

Mahi’s eyes grew wide with surprise and she stepped back. “The fountain is working today if you want to cool down immediately,” she said, without caring about his lousy behaviour.

Abhi sighed deeply. Mahi was his next-door neighbour. They were the same age, but she studied in a different school. She always carried a book in her hand. Her dusky complexion stood out in the pristine white dresses she always wore, and boys would frequently mock her as the ‘reading witch’.

Suddenly, a question based on Pulkit’s assessment crossed his mind. Mahi had left the park by then, but Abhi ran and caught up with her.

“Do girls like wicked, mean boys?” he asked.

Mahi gave such a peal of laughter that people

passing by turned to look at them. She clutched her belly and leaned on a nearby bench to avoid falling.

"Sure. Where did you get this idea?" she asked, still smirking.

"Just answer the question."

Noticing Abhi's seriousness, she sobered down a bit. "More than a person's preference, it is the personality and character of an individual that matters," she replied.

"Aah! You and your bookish quotes."

"Okay, hear me out. Every person is like a book. They are being governed by words and chapters, and new characters flit in and out of their life every day. Everyone may not connect with a book, but a book always finds its reader," she concluded.

"Mahi! I asked you one simple question."

"And I have answered beautifully, so kindly appreciate it."

Abhi threw his hand in the air out of frustration and started to walk away.

“Sometimes people are unable to choose you because they can’t see through you,” she said.

Abhi stopped and tried to understand what Mahi had just said.

“You have a good heart, Abhi. And if you are having to change yourself for someone to please them, then they don’t deserve you. They probably won’t stay with you for long either,” she said, shrugging her shoulders.

Abhi froze. How could Mahi relate to his question so much? Did somebody tell her what happened to him? He turned to look at her and noticed her smiling, innocent face. There was no way that a rumour could have reached another school. He knew she was intelligent. Instead of thinking more about her sound, complicated words, he took the easier way out and left.

5

The door shut on her face. Shalini slumped on the floor, her body drained of all energy. *Heartless devil,* these words echoed around her. And that too from her brother! As long as she could remember, she was best at everything – obedient daughter, class topper, and a great friend. Unlike her studious classmates, she would happily share notes with students who wanted them and they almost worshipped her.

But when your life is an open book, the boundary between personal and public preferences fades away. Getting assistance for yourself feels like a burden. When you help too much, you end up feeling more helpless.

Abhi was just a child. What he considered love was nothing but infatuation. Shalini understood that. Her brother had an emotional range. He would not take it well if his feelings were not reciprocated. She could sense the undertone of his spoken words, his voice drenched in suffering and anguish. She could not let this episode wound him for life. What a vicious circle! Though bewildered before, she slowly gained her composure and smiled with pain. No matter how hard she tried to protect her little brother, life always got in the way.

Limping slightly, she went to her room and looked at the almirah. There was something in there she had once decided never to look at. Her resolve slowly disintegrating, she pushed the clothes aside and pulled out a diary. With trembling fingers, she hugged it to her chest and opened it. There was a folded sheet of paper inside. Gathering her strength, she pulled the paper out and slowly unfolded it. When her eyes fell on the note, the date, and the handwriting, her heart skipped a beat. Remembering her brother, she regained her composure and started reading.

'I don't know where to begin. It seems as if we have already been together since the beginning. From childhood to adolescence to our youth – we have shared so many beautiful memories. We have spent so much time together that there is no need for me to say this. But now you have become extremely popular, and the circle is expanding. I am afraid that someone else might whisk you away if I don't say this in time.'

'I know you have limited patience so I won't bore you out. The only thing you can tolerate for long is a guitar. So I will say just this – Dev when you play, your fingers connect with your soul and the music flows in a melody that is rare and precious. The song we hear is not some composition but the sound of your beating heart... and that is what you are to me!'

Youth and tears have an unlikely relationship. When we are young, we can feel the emotions flowing out. As we grow old, weeping becomes a regular occurrence, so its novelty wears off. We could cry with or without them, nobody would notice.

6

The Internet is full of life. Keeping aside the never-ending debate of its merits and demerits, one cannot deny deriving pleasure from the infinite memes and funny videos available online. Every day, thousands of clips are being uploaded of failed efforts, deliberate attempts, accidents, falls, voice overs etc. on unusual incidents, morphing the actual context and its meaning. We scroll for hours, captivated by the sheer volume of content online, unable to let go. It's just like the effects of hallucinogenic drugs – providing either happiness or a means to escape from reality.

A lousy singer may have honest intentions and

would work hard as per their available resources. Yet we laugh at their effort. Why? Are we doing anything to help the individual? Sometimes, even after gaining popularity, the person continues to make random videos for the sake of views and shares and ends up getting sponsorships. Who has the last laugh then? Pretty ironic! We fail in so many ways every day, yet we enjoy watching someone else's failure – apparently, it's comforting. Mocking or judging others is a habit we neither identify with nor work upon. We have desensitised ourselves to such an extent that we have no idea of the torture that's inflicted on the individual we are mocking. If you are lucky, you will never become the victim of an Internet meme, or so we can argue. Well, in this case, Abhi was about to find out.

He received a message from Pulkit on Instagram. Someone had made a video of Kavya throwing the bouquet at him in front of the Taj Mahal. It was shared through a meme page account. The creator had added some music and graphics for a dramatic effect and titled the video 'Failed Majnu'. Completely winded, Abhi checked the numbers under the video – 25K views, 2500 comments. And this was just one account. The angle of the video was such that Kavya was hard to recognise. However, his face was clear as day. Whoever knew Abhi would know that the girl in question was Kavya.

He rifled through the comments. It appeared that laughing emojis were public's favourite. Others included 'poor fellow' 'What an idiot!' 'What was he smoking before he did this?' 'Should have had some decency, look at the poor girl's embarrassment'. The list went on and the trolls continued to pour in.

Abhi was shaking so much he had to find support to steady himself. His mind was still processing the day's events, and now this – he couldn't believe this was happening to him. He frantically scrolled through the incessant comments and was stunned at how fast the video had gone viral. What if his father saw this? And his relatives? They will never let him live this down. What about the neighbours? How will he face his peers at school? His teachers will find out about this for sure. And

Kavya? Oh gosh, how will Kavya react?

In his frenzy, he forgot about the phone's battery and it soon died down. He wanted to smash the phone on the sidewalk and make the video go away – if only that was possible. He started punching a tree next to him until a street dog intervened and he was forced to stop. The dog was a neighbourhood 'friendly' and would rouse the entire street if Abhi didn't stop. The evening faded in, and Abhi waited for the exact moment to strike before entering his home.

7

Fifteen minutes before dad arrived from work was the golden period to return home. Mom and Shalini would be busy with dinner and end-of-day chores. Abhi checked his watch for the opportune moment, then entered home, rushed to his room, and gently shut the door. He fell on the bed backwards, as if throwing himself from a cliff with his back facing oblivion, his eyes looking up at the sky.

Kavya was the love of his life. Why couldn't she see that? What went wrong and how? He knew that fate had brought her to him. Then how could this catastrophe happen? The first time he visited her home, it was supposed to be an hour's job. But the power outage made them wait for more than half a day and they had such a wonderful time together. They went out to eat and out of nowhere, it started to pour, making a splendid setting. Stuck where they were, they had no option but to talk endlessly, sharing every bit of their lives.

Gradually, he could sense her. Once, restless for no reason, he called her late at night only to discover that she was weeping uncontrollably – it was nostalgia for her previous city. They connected; he needed no proof. Those feelings, the desire, attachment, love – he had never felt like this before for anyone. It had all started with her, and it would end with her. She had to be a part of his life – it was fate. If her presence in his life was ordained, then why did she reject and leave him? He did not deserve such pain, humiliation, and suffering. He hadn't hurt so much as a fly in his entire life.

But it looked like destiny wanted to present him a harsh blow. What was he supposed to do now? How could he go to school? He couldn't stop himself and checked Instagram constantly. He remembered the time when he used to do this for leisure. Those countless idiots he had laughed at – he understood their pain now, both physical and mental. But this was not his fault. We set the premises for making fun look like this!

For the first time in his life, Abhi felt completely out of control. He behaved like a nervous wreck. He would cry and then be interrupted by periods of dry spells, as if the body no longer had the ability to vent. He had two options. One was to go meet Kavya and explain everything to her again. He was the perfect match for her; they were so compatible. The other was to keep quiet and ride out the humiliation of the video. This meant staying in his room and never getting out which was impossible. What would he say to his parents? The first option seemed more optimistic. He'd promise Kavya to keep her happy forever. She was his true love, after all. Love happens once in a lifetime and he would not let it go. Even though he had already said all this to her, he wanted to try once again. Maybe she got offended because of his revelation in a public place.

Whatever she thought, his choice of the proposal was perfect. She had mentioned on several occasions that she liked public displays of affection. She would argue that what is the point of a relationship wherein you can't express yourself freely, indoors or outdoors? And then when he actually proposed this way, she freaked out! What could be a better place to do it other than the symbol of love, the Taj Mahal?

Her parents were out of town, and Abhi decided to make things right in person. He had to explain himself. What if she was still thinking about him? They had spent numerous days and nights together; how could she withstand the suffocation of separation so effortlessly? He prayed that she'd take him back. Even if the world made fun of him, he could face it with elan if Kavya was by his side. However, if she rejected him again, he had only one option left – to never come back home again. His eyes misted at the thought of this idea. What would be the point of living when you are nothing but a joke in everyone's eye – seniors, juniors, classmates, teachers, relatives, family, friends, and the worst of the lot, parents?

He changed his clothes and got ready. Going out from the main door was impossible – he had to use the window. He turned around and stared at his room for a while, hoping that it wasn't for the last time.

8

Shalini entered the room with a plate of cheese sandwich and a mug of coffee, just the way her brother liked it. Abhi's head was so drowsy that he did not even notice the opening of the door, let alone the approaching footsteps.

"Whatever plot you are hatching, it will fail," she said, sitting next to him and placing a hand on his shoulder.

Abhi shook up from his reveries.

"One wrong word, and you will regret it," replied Abhi, his voice wavering slightly. Shalini calmly placed the food on the side table. She shut the door and walked up to Abhi. His eyes were wet with tears, one leg dangling outside the window. She tried to grab his arm and pull him inside, but Abhi retaliated, shoving her hand aside as he regained his balance.

Undeterred, Shalini grabbed her brother again and pulled him back inside the room. Abhi tried to struggle, but was devoid of all energy by then. Shalini stared at him for a second and then suddenly hugged him. Abhi froze. He wasn't expecting this reaction from her. She was no less than an enemy to him. For as long as he could remember, he had always ended up hating her. Even his friends disliked Shalini because she was nosy and interfering. The warmth of her embrace melted any remnants of resolve in him. He let out a cry and succumbed to his emotions. Shalini held him tight while tears and saliva drenched her shoulder. It was difficult for her to hold back and she too broke down, looking at the condition of her brother.

"It hurts, it hurts so much. My heart will burst

open. She… she said I should never meet her again. She said, I broke this relationship!"

Shalini made him sit on the bed. She held his hand while he wailed uncontrollably.

"My emotions are so pure. I prayed to God to make her mine. She is my life; she is my love. What will I do if I fail? True love only happens once in a lifetime," he said, continuing to sob in his sister's lap.

"And on top of that, there is a video of me being rejected floating around on social media. I am the joker of this town now. Do I deserve this humiliation? I am going to ask her one more time."

Shalini just stared at her brother dazedly and said, "You are her baggage-buddy."

Abhi lifted his head and gawked at her in confusion.

"One who is used out of convenience. A friend who fills times of loneliness, but is soon discarded when no longer needed. Such people become closer than normal friends, and it's quite easy to mistake them as your soulmate or someone who is very into you."

"Shut up! What do you know about –"

"Everything. That is what elder siblings are for. We have more experience in life."

"Aah! You will never change. For a moment, I thought you do have a little heart, but I was wrong. You are just a controlling fanatic!"

"Abhi, I checked her out. Whatever she did, it was not her fault. Whatever you are doing, it is also not wrong. Just look at your pain as a beautiful sentiment. It expands our threshold to experience the joy of love when it truly arrives in our life. Without this pain, you will never understand the depth of love."

"What is wrong with you? What are you babbling about?" said Abhi, failing to understand.

"Okay. Do you think this is your first love and that it has to be successful because you can only fall in love once?"

Abhi thought for a while. Being asked directly, he got a little confused, but he knew that deep down he did believe that.

"Where did you hear this? Movies, friends, social media?"

Abhi was silent.

"You know, mom and dad met each other in college and have been together since then. Are they any different from our neighbours who had an arranged marriage or any other similar couple?" Shalini's perspective pierced his grief and made him think.

"What is first love, Abhi? Tell me. One that makes you misunderstand or which loves you back but breaks up after a while? How about one that reciprocates your feelings and stays with you through thick and thin? Aren't all of these first for their own reasons?"

Shalini's discourse crumbled Abhi's views, but the words would have had a better impact if they weren't hers. She was the last person Abhi would listen to or find convincing. Her daily actions were the exact opposite of how she was behaving today. What did she know about love? Despite being a topper or having a huge friend circle, she was still a lonely, irritating, elder sibling with no social media presence. All she had done was torment him his entire life, and now suddenly she wanted to preach.

"You are a love guru now? What do you even know about this emotion?" said Abhi with exasperation. Shalini knew Abhi would react this way. We all make mistakes, and this was her biggest one – failing to recognise that her brother was all grown up. Yes, she was hard on him, but it was to protect him. She should have changed her behaviour and treated him with respect. He was not a kid anymore who would just do as he was told. The way he had pushed her in the morning was not a joke. His words 'heartless devil' were still ringing in her ears. They had the potential to ruin his future relationships. The emotion she had witnessed today was beyond anger — it was hate. She understood Abhi's vulnerability. He was in love, a rare occurrence in today's generation. With countless dating apps just one click away, easy hook-ups had become the new normal and the novelty of true love was all but dead. Looking at Abhi, she had not witnessed such intensity in a long time. Why couldn't he be more like the kids his age?

"... and despite all of it, I am the *joke*. Someone made a video of my proposal and the meme has gone viral. How can I face the world now? Only if Kavya accepts me, everything will be alright. If not, I don't want to live anymore."

Shalini was stunned. Her brother was thinking of ending his life. She had watched the video. It was definitely a hit with the masses and was being actively circulated under the entertainment section. She realised her words weren't hitting home with Abhi. The letter was her last resort. She wasn't going to berate him for his thoughts or actions. Rather, she would empathise with him and gently shoulder him out of his pain. The mere touch of the paper tugged at her heart again, as if it was just written and delivered. She brought it out and slowly handed it over to her brother.

Abhi unfolded it and started to read. At first, it was difficult for him to comprehend the words, but when he came across the name 'Dev', he understood. It was his sister's love letter! He knew the boy; Dev was extremely popular. He also knew that Shalini had helped her best friend Harshita get together with Dev – they were dating now. The trio were still friends and Abhi disliked Dev because he always praised his sister, but now he understood.

He noticed the grief in Shalini's eyes but her smile said it all.

"All this time? Did you even tell him?" asked Abhi.

"Words are the illusion of communication. True understanding comes only when we can feel each other. And if he didn't feel this way, then there was no point in telling him. I know it sounds dramatic, but I chose to wait. To see what life has in store for me. There is so much to discover and experience."

"But you have adored him since childhood. He was your first love!"

"My little brother, life is not about loving once or twice. It is about the experience, and the innumerable attempts at finding your perfect partner. So don't hurt yourself so much. The truth is, you have a long life ahead of you. You will find your soulmate one day. After all, my brother is so handsome and likeable, who wouldn't want him?" said Shalini with a smile.

"The joke, the meme, have you forgotten?"

"People do not care about anything except themselves. You watch hundreds of memes every day. Do you remember all of them? Yes, your classmates will make fun of you. Yes, you failed, but who hasn't? People will talk for some time and then they'll forget. If you don't let their words bother you, they will forget even sooner."

Abhi beamed. He could not believe he was having this conversation with his devil sister. The concept of first love, true love, and many loves reflected in love songs and movies is completely different from what he was experiencing. What Shalini had done was one of the bravest things ever – surrendering her childhood love for the sake of her best friend. He forgot about himself for a while and tried to imagine what Shalini would have gone through, and was still going through since she hung out with Dev and Harshita every day.

His concept of love had completely meddled, but it was too exhausting to grasp it right away. He ate the sandwich, drank the coffee, and lay down on his bed. Convinced that Abhi had calmed down, Shalini left his room, her mind flooding with a rush of memories. However, this time there was happiness emanating in her heart – the wound of one, a lesson for the other.

9

When we are young, small incidents feel like the end of the world. For a child, a broken toy is a tragedy that calls for excessive weeping. For a youngster, heartbreak feels the same way. Fortunately or unfortunately, with age we understand that these incidents are just a part of life. Classifying them as major or minor is utterly inconsequential as they are all important because of the feelings one attaches to them. However, nothing compares to the pain we experience when our hearts are pure, or are a little less polluted by worldly malice.

Abhi's heartbreak shattered him as expected – it was a classic textbook case. His range of emotions was somehow depleted, and he became numb. Sudden bursts of tears, staring at the wall, forgetting to eat, unable to react – his actions were beyond his control. Shalini helped him by creating a fake medical certificate so he could ditch school for a few days.

Her argument was logical, but Abhi was yet to comprehend the conversation. There was no point in listening if you refused to understand. Abhi not only had to pay heed to her words, but act on them too.

He re-read his messages to Kavya, slowly and steadily. He looked at their photos and eventually noticed a pattern. He would jump if he received a notification from Kavya on any of the social media platforms. That excitement soon began to fade away. Those calls for help, long conversations into the night seemed to be pretty one-sided, all depending on Kavya's mood. So many times she would reply to his messages the next day, saying she was busy or had slept off. He had been blinded by her charm and aura. Was he really a 'baggage-buddy'? All these feelings he had for her, were they imaginary? Apparently, it wasn't cupid that had brought them together.

All these thoughts drummed in his head. What is a person left with if all his beliefs are draining away? Abhi got out of bed, changed his clothes, and went for a walk, leaving his phone behind.

A rock-like heaviness floated above his head and each step was an effort. He kept his eyes on the road and trudged along. The weather was dry and highly unpleasant. He was quite uncomfortable but accepted his physical discomfort as a welcome distraction – anything was better than the anxiety plaguing his mind. Subconsciously, he turned towards the park and ended up sitting on a bench with no intention of resting. The burning seat added to his apprehensiveness, and he started sweating profusely.

Someone came and stood beside him. Abhi noticed the person looking down at him – conversation was the last thing he wanted. He looked up and saw Mahi smiling at him.

"Here," she said, handing him a bottle of chilled water.
Abhi shook his head and refused to take it.

"You don't seem like your usual self," said Mahi, gleefully. When she didn't get an answer, she sat on the bench, folded her legs, pulled out a book from her handbag, and started to read. The murmuring and frequent page-turning interfered with his need for silence. They sat like that for quite some time.

The vacuum created by the heat started to fade, and the wind started to blow, gradually drying his sweat. Suddenly the wind swept a flower towards their bench; it landed between the book's open pages. Mahi picked it up and turned towards Abhi. "This is for you," she said.

Lost in his thoughts, Abhi turned and was embarrassed by Mahi's public gesture. He stared at her. She was looking at him platonically, as calm as the blowing wind. Ignoring her actions, he started to leave.

"I should be going," said Abhi.

Mahi grasped his hand and made him sit.

"So, Mr Popular, now that you have become famous, you won't accept flowers from girls?" she asked, giggling.

Mahi was just kidding, but Abhi was unable to differentiate that from mocking.

"I know how you must be feeling. I understand why you asked me that question the other day. I saw your video online. But let me tell you, that was one hell of a romantic attempt. To be honest, I was quite surprised to see the 'Romeo' hidden inside you."

"What is the point? I still got rejected and have now become the laughing-stock of the town."

"People who break are the ones that stand the tallest."

"You and your bookish rubbish," said Abhi, standing up in frustration.

"Well, if my future boyfriend does not get this

creative, I am not saying yes," she said, winking. "I'm confused. I don't understand girls at all. Like, are you being honest or making fun of me? I have no clue," he said, pressing his temples to alleviate his building headache. "Tell me one thing, had I asked you out in the same way, would you have said yes? Answer me!"

"Sure, why not?" replied Mahi.

Abhi gawked at her. She was not the type to bluff and looked very serious at that moment.

"Abhi, love is a lot more than acceptance or rejection. I believe that there is a time and place for everything. So yes, for me, now is the time to do well in school. But what is wrong in saying yes to such a beautiful feeling? It would have become an interesting chapter in the book of my life."

Abhi stared at her in disbelief. Such difference of opinions. Kavya lambasted him for all his effort, and she did not even care to keep her voice down before lashing out insults. And then there was Mahi, with an altogether different and broader perspective. For the first time since the incident, he had met someone who was reacting to him positively and sharing a similar viewpoint. His friend Pulkit had quoted his proposal as 'hyper-romantic', 'breakup plan', 'giving girls a gastric disorder', 'suicide mission', and whatnot!

"You are an idiot, but an intelligent one," said Abhi with a smile. He slumped on the bench, letting his head fall back.

"So I did put that smile back on your face," said Mahi, and they both laughed. Mahi offered her water bottle again and this time Abhi drank it till the last drop.

He glanced at Mahi from the corner of his eye. She didn't need to make an effort to convince him that she meant well, that she would be there in times of need. This feeling overwhelmed him as he had never experienced it with Kavya. His head started to ring with Shalini's words. His beliefs cracked.

10

Out of concern, Mr Sharma asked Abhi to ditch the school bus and personally dropped him at school. Abhi was quiet the entire time, his eyes glued at the road. A whirlwind of emotions was passing through him. He took a deep breath before stepping out of the car and entered the school with his signature smile.

He timed his arrival to avoid the usual early morning chit-chat in class and directly joined the school assembly. The classes began, and he found teachers glancing at him periodically. During recess, he approached his peers and jested with them. He only received sarcastic comments in return. Even students from other classes, both seniors and juniors – sniggered behind his back when they identified him from the meme video.

Abhi concentrated on his studies as the day progressed, raising queries and answering questions with enthusiasm, but the jokes refused to cease. 'I messed up, bro', 'Yes, I am an idiot', 'Well, I was dumb and blind', he kept repeating, affirming his mistake. Before anyone could make fun of him, he made fun of himself. By the end of the day, Abhi was exhausted with this charade. Still, things were better than he had expected.

When school was over, Abhi hid in the library for some time, waiting for everyone to leave. As soon as he stepped out, Pulkit joined him.

"You have earned so much respect today. It is not easy," said Pulkit, hugging him. "How did you bounce back after falling so hard? How did you manage to keep taking those shots?"

"I guess I had some support," replied Abhi, keeping his face down and trying to maintain his emotional balance.

"You outdid yourself, but you cannot hide from me, you idiot."

Abhi was amused at his friend's ribbing. Finally, he smiled.

"These girls –"

"No buddy, it is about an individual. Boy or girl, both can be inconsiderate," said Abhi.

"Whoa, what a transformation!" said Pulkit, kicking a stone. A person halted the rock's toppling. The moment he looked at the obstruction, Pulkit wished he had aimed higher, so it could have hit the head. It was Kavya waiting.

#

Kavya had had her share of hardships. She was still not accustomed to moving from one city to another, that was a mandate in her father's job. No matter what people say about 'keeping in touch', they will always forget you, eventually. Memories are nothing but baggage, and losing them is difficult. This was her third city since she could remember, and changing schools was the biggest headache. Meeting new people and building relationships from scratch was irksome as it was just a wasted effort. The truth is, everything is temporary.

People, time, situations, habits, commitments, emotions, everything changes. This is what her life experiences had taught her, which is why she was afraid of anything 'permanent' in her life. She knew people did not like her. She didn't care to change their opinion because she would move on soon, so it was not worth the effort. Her being the centre of attraction made it easier for her to cope. Kavya had no qualms in rejecting boys – she noticed their fake words and baseless emotions, so it was easy to do so. Someone once told her that she always had a strange smile on her face whenever she rejected somebody's token of love.

But in Abhi's case, she felt a strange pang of guilt and immense frustration. She knew how he felt, because he never disappointed her. He had always kept his feelings in check. He was her exact opposite, believing in permanency as opposed to temporary endeavours. His conversations included too many words like 'lifetime' and 'forever'. He was quite handy though, solving all her problems and easing out her troubles. Her friends mocked at her for using him. Was it her fault that Abhi wanted to be used? Despite all this, she knew her reaction that day was uncalled for and that she should have treated him with respect. She *did* want their connection to last a little longer.

But that viral video ruined everything. The fraction of warmth she felt towards him evaporated and all she wanted to do was to take him back to the Taj Mahal and slap the daylights out of him. When she went to school, she was surprised to find herself at the receiving end of taunts and jokes. Instead of sympathising, the classmates and students were making fun of her. She became lonelier.

Despite *their* incident, Kavya expected Abhi to call her, asking for forgiveness for his behaviour. That would have given her the perfect opportunity to give him a piece of her mind. She waited for a week, facing ridicule at school all by herself. Abhi was missing for that entire time and when he finally came to school, he was happier than ever. There were no signs of embarrassment or sadness on his face. It was like the incident never happened. She couldn't believe how unfazed he was. Worse, he didn't even look at her and kept his distance, clearly avoiding her.

"Just when I thought things were going well," said Pulkit, walking ahead while Abhi stood still.

Kavya approached Abhi.

"You stained our relationship, turned me into a joke, generated all this negative publicity, didn't have the decency to message me, came back after a week to strut about, and still have the gall to ignore me?" screamed Kavya.

Abhi's heart pounded in his chest as she spoke. Every word, every letter launched an attack at the mental guards he had created.

"I need an answer Abhi, what were you thinking? First you took me to that stupid monument and blabbered all that rubbish, and now by acting indifferent, what are you trying to prove?"

Rubbish? His guards were about to fall.

"You ruined a healthy friendship, and now –"

"Every person is like a book. They are being governed by words and chapters, and new characters flit in and out of their life every day. Not everyone connects with a book, and not every book is for a reader. Your chapter simply ended." said Abhi.

"What?"

Abhi walked away, extending the courtesy of one last glance at Kavya. There stood the person who he loved the most, blaming him for everything, and he took it. He still wanted to apologise to her, but it was meaningless now. Mahi's dialogue saved him from breaking down, but deep inside, everything shattered. Had Kavya expressed even a modicum of emotion or understanding, he would have forgotten everything and tried to patch up with her, but there was nothing. He was wrong. There was no connection between him and Kavya, not like he had with Mahi. Letting go is considered a failure. 'Keep trying' is the internationally accepted lesson. At times, your heart may guide you if you listen to it carefully and let it. It may also give you random hints of when to stop and when to leave. Abhi took a deep breath and left.

Pulkit accompanied him till the school bus and then left. "Abhi bhaiya, why were you crying in front of your girlfriend in the video?" asked Atul, a boy from fifth grade. Everyone in the bus roared with laughter. The driver glanced at Abhi and yelled at the kids, silencing them at once. Abhi was sitting in the pilot seat right next to the driver. He opened the window to his left and pushed his face out. Hot winds lashed at him, calming his mind and hiding the grief bubbling inside him.

When coursing through life, there are days that are pivotal for growth and development. Every milestone has a before and an after, but the change it brings is permanent. Abhi could sense his heart hardening and his resolve becoming stronger to face the uncertain future with grace and maturity.

This incident, the memories, his shattered dream would ache for sure. But all these experiences taught him one of the biggest lessons of life – he knew love, and he knew loss.

Change Stories – Next Reads

Kuroopa

'Why did God make me so ugly? Am I not your daughter? Was I exchanged at the hospital? Or did you leave me in the sun one day and that's why I became so dark?'

Meera, one of three siblings, has been struggling with her identity since childhood. She is subjected to mean, insensitive remarks by neighbours, relatives, and random people around her due to the lack of pleasing physical attributes. Constant comparison with her fair, blue-eyed sister further deteriorates her relationship with friends, family, and most importantly, herself.

A shocking incident involving the household pets pushes Meera over the edge, forcing her parents, especially her father, to take action and bring her back to reality.

Will Meera be able to find her footing in this hypocritical world that preaches "looks don't matter" while constantly objectifying and running towards beautification? Will she be able to accept herself for who she is and overcome the hatred she has for herself?

A Gutterful Life

Hindus and Muslims live in harmony across an open gutter (naala) at the edge of the city.

Whether it's the story of Somu and Aklaq – two innocent souls from different religions who stumble into each other on the naala and foster a friendship like no other; Billu and Arif – two budding businessmen trying to make a living – who are subjected to inter-community politics through the tryst of fate; or the community's favourite Chai-Chachu – an old tea-seller with unknown origin but an important story to tell, *A Gutterful Life* brings forth a plethora of sentiments culminating in an emotional climax.

Will Aklaq and Somu's friendship survive the vagaries of communal division? Will Chai-Chachu be able to bridge the gap between Hindus and Muslims across the naala? Will religious propaganda compel people to forget their hardships and sow seeds of division in the illusion of unity?

Flying With Chains

Three friends – Yatin, Taruni, and Kunal – have been joined at the hip since childhood. They live close by, go to the same school, and always hang out at the same rendezvous. As they grow up, their parents become uncomfortable about their closeness and try to keep them apart.

Whether it's Yatin's struggle to clear the civil services examination, Kunal's difficulty in convincing his businessman father to let him pursue physics, or Taruni's rebellion to break free from the shackles of patriarchy, undue expectations from friends and family builds the pressure on this trio.

Will their friendship withstand the test of time or will the demands of society unravel their relationship and lead to mistrust and betrayal? Will they be able to chase their dreams or will they succumb to their inevitable fate?

A Mother By The Window

'A final lesson for her, she thought. A woman's happiness resides outside herself, in places defined by society.'

Neetu, an obedient housewife, devotes all her time and energy to take care of her family. She is diligent and abides by the rules society has laid out for her. Nostalgia of winning a beauty pageant many years ago and regret of marrying early encourages her to try her hand at becoming an influencer on Instagram.

She works hard to achieve her new goal, without disrupting the life she was married into. Her attention eventually gets divided between her dream and family, bringing to light the secret she is harbouring. The secret hurts her image of an "ideal wife" much to her husband's chagrin.

With Neetu's life in turmoil, Rahul takes a stand to save his mother's dream.

Will Neetu realise her true potential and achieve her dream? Are women expected to fulfil only one role at a time, and no other? Does a woman's personal life belong only to her family? Is there any hope for change?

Also by

Kapil Raj

Now, a national bestseller.

Life was a fun fed roller coaster: new found love, drugs, cat-fights, patch ups, crushes, night hangouts, and unplanned trips. Like any girl, not in the wildest dream, palak could imagine that after attending a rave party, she will wake up to the horror of finding herself raped.

In traumatic conditions and struggle between sanity and hallucinations, she is compelled by the circumstances to leave her world. Already fighting a war within, her stances take a toll witnessing horrifying tales of women and girls. Little did she know that this catastrophe was not enough for one lifetime, and a storm — was just cooling its heels.

Will she be able to carve her path while facing the rapists, her tyrant father, appearances of her passed away mother? Should palak let her life to be decided by people, society, and taboos? Would justice return her life or revenge lend her peace?

A heart-rending story of a girl, whose beliefs and honor has been battered, stands up to make choices, rediscovering the meaning of life.

About the Author

Kapil Raj is a professional, speaker and writer-activist based in Delhi-NCR, India. With the heart of a philosopher, mind of a realist, and a deep-rooted non-conformist, he lives many lives, yet stealing the time for the most precious thing that matters to him: crafting plots, playing with characters, and weaving the stories based on intricate social subjects and challenging the dogmas.

His debut novel *ENDURER A Rape Story* is critically acclaimed by the media and loved by the readers. He is a noted speaker and delivered lectures in prestigious institutions and colleges.

Connect with him on Facebook, Twitter, Instagram @ikapilraj